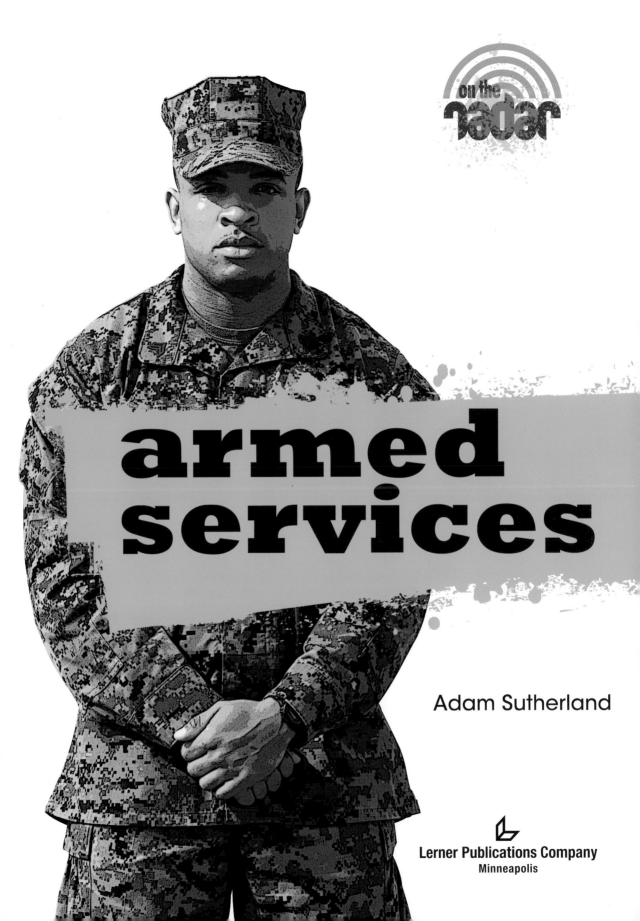

armed services

Adam Sutherland

Lerner Publications Company
Minneapolis

First American edition published in 2012
by Lerner Publishing Group, Inc.
Published by arrangement with Wayland, a division of Hachette Children's Books

Lerner Publications Company
A division of Lerner Publishing Group, Inc.
241 First Avenue North
Minneapolis, MN U.S.A.

Website address: www.lernerbooks.com

Library of Congress Cataloging-in-Publication Data

Sutherland, Adam.
   Armed services / by Adam Sutherland.
      p.   cm. — (On the radar: defend and protect)
   Includes index.
   ISBN 978-0-7613-7771-9 (lib. bdg. : alk. paper)
   1. United States—Armed Forces—Juvenile literature. 2. Military art and science—Juvenile literature. I. Title.
UA23.S9425 2012
355.00973—dc23   2011023219

Manufactured in the United States of America
- CG - 12/31/11

Acknowledgments: Alamy: Newsphoto 22–23; Flickr: MashleyMorgan 20–21; iStockphoto: MTMCOINS 1; Royal Navy: 2bl, 9r, 17t, 24–25; Shutterstock: Zagibalov Aleksandr 3br, 30–31, Daniel Alvarez 8b, Gary Blakeley 12l, Hung Chung Chih 26b, Homeros 13r, Andrii Kravchenko 2tr, 13l, Stephen Meese, 29l, Byron W. Moore 11l, Regien Paassen 0t, Losevsky Pavel 26–27, Laurin Rinder 2br, 19, Studio 37 cover, Tatonka back cover, Oleg Zabielin 6–7, 31b; U.S. Army: 2tl, 4–5, 14–15, 14, 16–17, 26t, 29l; Wikipedia: U.S. Armed Forces 12r; © Dario Bajurin/Dreamstime.com, 29c.

Main body text set in Helvetica Neue LT Std 13/15.5.
Typeface provided by Adobe Systems.

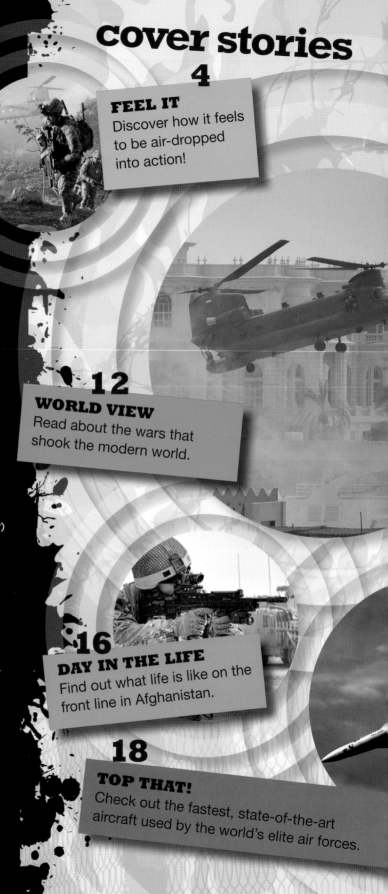

cover stories

the people

the machines

the moves

the talk

INTO ACTION!

Last night I stood on guard duty for two hours, squinting through a night-sight device. Just had time to grab an hour's sleep, but now everyone is on red alert. This is what we have been working toward for months, right back to basic training. Before dawn breaks, the Chinook and Apache helicopters are standing by, ready to take us deep behind enemy lines.

INTO THE UNKNOWN

We sit side by side on the choppers. The rattle of equipment and the buzz of the rotor blades cut through the air. Talking is useless. It's easier to use hand signals—gestures we learned in basic training and respond to automatically. My throat is as dry as a desert; nerves or excitement, I'm not sure which. I'm ready to go. I want to go. I just don't know what to expect. A firefight or a complete surrender? There's no way of knowing until we get there.

COMBAT READY

It's time for takeoff. The adrenaline surges through my body, and my pulse starts to race. What will we see when we land? Whatever it is, we have to be ready for it. We're landing outside a rebel-held stronghold. We're not doing this quietly, so everyone will hear us coming. We're in the air for 20 minutes. When we land, the training kicks in. Our bodies do what they need to do, and our brains barely sense the danger. It's amazing what you can teach yourself.

BEHIND ENEMY LINES

We're down. The doors open. The noise of the rotors gets louder and almost unbearable. It's mixed with the shouts of the commanding officers and the heavy thud of hundreds of boots hitting the ground running. It's my turn now. Wish me luck. I might need it.

THE FORCES

The armed services are a country's military forces. They can be sent anywhere in the world—sometimes to fight but often to stop conflicts between other countries and groups. Each service has its own ranks, its own special duties and skills, and its own uniforms and equipment.

THE ARMY

The U.S. Army is our land-based military force. Since the end of World War II (1939–1945), the size of the world's armies has shrunk dramatically as equipment and training have both improved. For example, the United States currently has 1.4 million people in its armed services. But during World War II, it had a massive 11 million recruits.

THE NAVY

Naval forces on ships, in submarines, and in navy aircraft patrol the world's oceans and seas. They defend their countries from attack. U.S. Navy vessels are often sent to areas of conflict to support our army and to provide floating headquarters for fellow armed services.

THE AIR FORCE

The U.S. Air Force uses fighter planes, helicopters, and other aircraft to fight enemies, to bomb targets on the ground, and to transport troops to battle zones.

The air force also helps to keep the peace by patrolling trouble spots. This branch of the military can deliver lifesaving supplies or help to get people out of danger zones.

THE MARINES

The U.S. Marine Corps works closely with the U.S. Navy to seize or defend naval bases during military campaigns. But the Corps performs in many areas. The Marines also participate in land operations as needed. Marine fighter pilots are some of the most skilled in the service. And the Marines guard U.S. embassies around the world.

THE COAST GUARD

The U.S. Coast Guard is the smallest branch of the U.S. armed forces. The main jobs of the Coast Guard are to patrol U.S. waters for illegal activity and to help when people or property at sea are in danger. To do these jobs, Coast Guard members may fight fires or use search-and-rescue equipment. The Coast Guard is often first on the spot during a natural disaster.

WAR OF WORDS!

Armed services have their own language. We have lifted the lid on the lingo to give you an insight.

Allies
the countries—including Britain, the United States, and the Soviet Union—that fought against the Axis in World War II. Also countries linked to the United States after the war

Axis
the countries—including Germany, Italy, and Japan—that fought against the Allies in World War II

battalion
300 to 1,000 soldiers, or the equivalent of three to five platoons

brigade
3,000 to 5,000 soldiers under the command of a colonel

civilian
a person who is not in the armed services

Cold War
an intense rivalry between the United States and the Soviet Union that started after World War II and ended in the 1990s

corps
20,000 to 45,000 soldiers, or the equivalent of two to five divisions

division
10,000 to 15,000 soldiers, or the equivalent of three brigades

enlisted soldiers
members of the armed services who are not officers

front line
the most advanced position occupied by an army

infantry
soldiers who are specially trained to fight on foot

Kevlar
a light, strong material used in army clothing

mercenaries
skilled soldiers hired and paid to fight in the service of a foreign country

night sight
a device that uses special technology to allow a user to see in the dark

platoon
16 to 44 soldiers, led by a lieutenant, equivalent to two to four squads

reconnaissance
the process of obtaining information about an enemy's position

reunified
reunited, or became one country again

rotor blades
the long, flat blades on top of a helicopter that make it fly

stealth capacity
the ability to avoid being spotted by enemy radar

theater of operations
an area in which active military operations are taking place, usually commanded by a high-ranking general

smoke grenades
grenades that let out smoke and are used for signaling to aircraft to mark landing zones

stronghold
an area that one army has complete control of and that is easy to defend

withdrawal of troops
the removal of troops, usually gradually, from a battle zone

squad
9 to 10 soldiers, the smallest element in the U.S. Army, led by a sergeant or staff sergeant

This image of helicopters leaving a military ship's deck at night was taken with a night-sight device.

GLOSSARY

adrenaline
a hormone found in the human body that causes the heart to beat faster

debris
rubble or fragments of something that has been destroyed, such as a building

supersonic
faster than the speed of sound

ceiling
height above which a plane will not work well

morale
happiness or positive mental state

coalition
a group formed temporarily because of shared needs

multinational
made up of groups from several different countries

Taliban
an Islamic movement whose military took control of Afghanistan in early 1995. The movement was forcibly removed from power by the United States and its allies after the September 11, 2001, attacks.

Communist
a person who believes in the Communist system of government in which the state plans and controls the economy

al-Qaeda
a terrorist network that targets the United States and its allies

stamina
the ability to keep doing something for a long time

United Nations
an international organization formed to keep peace among the world's nations

WAR OF AGES

Small groups of trained, full-time soldiers have been around for thousands of years. But only in the last 400 years have countries been able to afford full-time military protection.

Roman soldiers held shields above their heads and in front of them to form a wall. This wall protected them from their enemies' weapons.

ANCIENT ARMIES

The Spartans in ancient Greece were one of the earliest professional armies. At seven, young boys were sent to live in barracks to train as soldiers. They devoted their lives to the service of their country until they retired at 60 years old. The ancient Roman army was made up of men who were required to serve for a certain number of years. In around 115 B.C., it became a professional army made up of Roman citizens who served for 25 years before being allowed to retire.

FIGHTING FOR MONEY

In the Middle Ages (A.D. 500 to 1500), many countries couldn't afford to pay full-time armies, so they hired mercenaries. These were professional soldiers who were hired to fight battles during times of conflict. By the seventeenth century, most countries had permanent armies.

BEST OF BRITISH

The British Army was formed in 1707, when the English and Scottish armies were united. During the eighteenth century, the British Army fought important wars against France, Scotland, and the American colonies. The Napoleonic Wars (1803–1815) against France caused the army to grow rapidly from 40,000 men in 1793 to 250,000 by 1813.

Unlike ancient armies, most modern armies include women in all services.

U.S. ARMED FORCES

The American Continental Army, led by George Washington, was formed to fight against Britain in the Revolutionary War (1775–1783). During the U.S. Civil War (1861–1865), the U.S. (or Union) army fought against the Southern (or Confederate) forces. More than 600,000 Americans from both sides died in the fighting. Conflicts with Mexico, Spain, and Native American nations continued in the late 1800s. In 1917 the United States took part in World War I (1914–1918), its first multinational war effort.

Modern-day warfare

The United States came into its own as a military superpower during and after World War II. The Cold War (1945–1991) against the other superpower—the then Soviet Union (modern Russia)—was played out in the Korean War (1950–1953) and the Vietnam War (1957–1975). With the breakup of the Soviet Union in 1991, the United States was the remaining military superpower. Since the 1990s, most of its military activities have been in coalition forces in Bosnia, Iraq, and Afghanistan.

GLOBAL CONFLICTS

A monument in Washington, D.C. *(left)*, marks the contribution of U.S. forces in World War II. The dense jungles of Vietnam made fighting against North Vietnamese troops extremely difficult for U.S. soldiers *(above)*.

Wars happen when one country invades another or when two countries disagree about each other's actions or beliefs. With more sophisticated weapons, modern wars may be shorter, but keeping the peace can be just as hard as winning a war.

THE WORLD AT WAR

With more than 100 million soldiers involved, World War II was the largest war in history. The Allies (mainly the United States, Britain, and the Soviet Union) fought the Axis (Germany, Japan, and Italy). The war began in September of 1939 and ended in 1945. World War II saw the United States and the Soviet Union emerge as the world's two superpowers. At the same time, countries worldwide joined together to form the United Nations.

WAR IN ASIA

The Vietnam War lasted from 1957 to 1975. It was a conflict between the Communist North (supported mainly by China and the Soviet Union) and the anti-Communist South (supported mainly by the United States). The war spread to surrounding countries, including Laos and Cambodia. The war ended when North Vietnam captured the South's capital city of Saigon (modern Ho Chi Minh City). The two countries were reunified the following year.

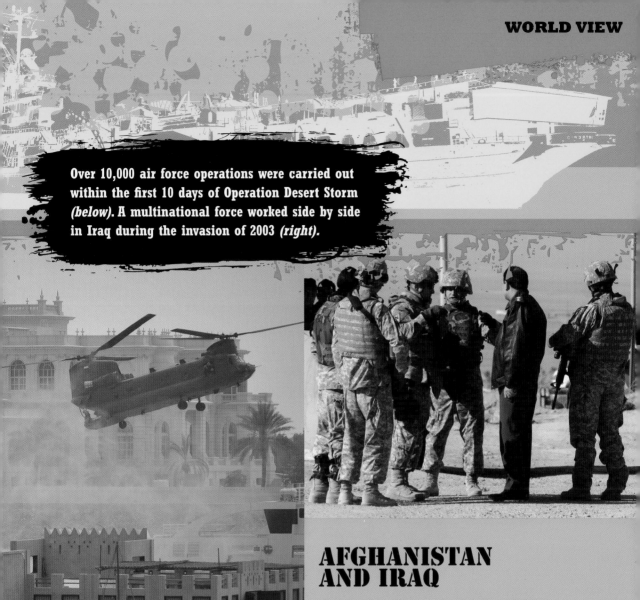

Over 10,000 air force operations were carried out within the first 10 days of Operation Desert Storm *(below).* A multinational force worked side by side in Iraq during the invasion of 2003 *(right).*

OPERATION DESERT STORM

When Iraq invaded Kuwait in August 1990, countries such as the United States, Britain, Saudi Arabia, and Egypt formed a coalition to force out Iraqi troops. Operation Desert Storm began with the aerial bombing of Iraqi forces in January 1991, followed by a ground assault the next month. Iraqi troops retreated just 100 hours after the ground campaign began.

AFGHANISTAN AND IRAQ

Starting in 2001, a multinational force was sent to Afghanistan to root out al-Qaeda terrorists and to remove the ruling Taliban from power. By 2011 more than 100,000 U.S. soldiers were stationed in Afghanistan. Plans are under way to reduce that number over the next several years. Meanwhile, in 2003, another mulitinational force invaded Iraq. Its then president Saddam Hussein was said to be building illegal nuclear weapons and funding terrorism. Hussein was captured, and the new Iraqi government tried and executed him. Thousands of U.S. troops are still stationed in Iraq. Full withdrawal is planned for 2015.

RANK AND FILE

The U.S. Army is divided into three groups. Enlisted people join at the lowest rank as privates. Noncommissioned officers (NCOs) are usually enlisted men or women who have been promoted to corporal or sergeant. Commissioned officers have the most authority. Officers at each level oversee units of soldiers. The number of soldiers under their command increases with their rank. The lowest rank of lieutenant oversees a platoon. Captains lead companies. Colonels oversee battalions and brigades, with majors often serving as their executive officers. Generals command a division, a corps, or an entire theater of operations.

LIEUTENANT GENERAL

The lieutenant general commands units of 20,000 to 45,000 soldiers.

GENERAL

A general usually has over 30 years of military experience and is the senior level of commissioned officer.

COLONEL

The colonel commands units of 3,000 to 5,000 soldiers.

CAPTAIN

The captain commands units of 64 to 190 soldiers.

SERGEANT

A sergeant usually commands a squad of around 10 soldiers. The sergeant supervises the privates' daily routines and sets an example for discipline, hard work, and professional behavior.

CORPORAL

The first rank of NCOs, corporals act as team leaders of the smallest army units and are responsible for soldiers' individual training and personal appearance.

PRIVATE

This is the army's lowest rank and is given to new recruits when they start basic combat training. A private's role is simple—to follow orders!

A SOLDIER'S LIFE IN AFGHANISTAN

MAJOR RUSSELL LEWIS

FRIDAY, JUNE 10, 2011

5:30 A.M. The sun's up, but it's still cool. A few of us head to the improvised gym—some free weights and a dirt running track—for 30 minutes of exercise. After that, it's into the solar-powered shower. This is basically a hosepipe, but the water is warmish, and there's plenty of it because we have our own well. We shave every day too—army rules!

7 A.M. Breakfast is served. We have our own cook, and all meals are prepared in the camp. Every two or three weeks, helicopters bring in fresh supplies of eggs, bread, and breakfast cereal. Once that's disappeared, we're back to canned food. Breakfast is oatmeal or beans, powdered eggs, and canned sausages.

8 A.M.–12 P.M. I spend my morning planning patrols, sending reports back to base, and walking around the camp, talking to the men and checking on morale. Our tour of duty lasts for six months. We have a lot of young soldiers, some as young as 18, so contact and communication are important.

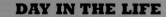

Daily routines include guard
duty, patrolling the local area,
and training—either at the firing
range or practicing first-aid skills.

12 P.M. Lunchtime. During the summer months, the temperature rises
to 113–122°F (45–50°C), so after eating, the men head to their bunks
with a book to escape the heat and to recharge their batteries. When
you're out on patrol, engaging with the enemy, carrying a 88-pound
(40-kilogram) bag on your back, it's mentally and physically exhausting.
You need to rest!

5 P.M. Dinnertime. We eat with our friends in small groups—usually pastas
or stews. These are all simple dishes that can easily be cooked with
canned food.

6 P.M. I get my staff together to review the day and make plans for
tomorrow. We discuss administration issues such as which parts of the
camp need cleaning up or more serious stuff such as a firefight with the
enemy.

7 P.M. It's getting dark now, and the men head for their bunks.
We watch films on mini-DVD players or read by flashhlight. We go
to sleep early as we're up at 5:30 A.M. tomorrow to do it all again!

COMBAT AIRCRAFT

The world's air forces fly the latest aircraft into battle. Here are some of the fastest, most expensive, and best-equipped aircraft in the world. Take a look to see how they compare.

C-130J SUPER HERCULES

A long-range transport plane used by the U.S. Air Force and Britain's Royal Air Force (RAF)

Wingspan: 132 feet (40.23 m)

Length: 98 feet (30 m)

Maximum speed: 417 mph (671 kph)

Ceiling: 28,000 feet (8,534 m)

Crew: 3

Cost: $62 million

F/A-18E SUPER HORNET

A supersonic fighter-bomber used by the U.S. Navy, the U.S. Air Force, and the U.S. Marines

Wingspan: 45 feet (13.7 m)

Length: 60 feet (18.4 m)

Maximum speed: 1,190 mph (1,915 kph)

Ceiling: 50,000 feet (15,240 m)

Crew: 1

Cost: $55 million

F-35 LIGHTNING II

Still in design, a ground attack and stealth plane to be used by the U.S. Air Force

Wingspan: 35 feet (10.65 m)

Length: 51.4 feet (15.6 m)

Maximum speed: 1,200 mph (1,931 kph)

Ceiling: 60,000 feet (18,288 m)

Crew: 1

Cost: $122 million

EF2000 EUROFIGHTER TYPHOON

A European-designed fighter plane used by the RAF, Germany, Italy, Spain, and Austria

Wingspan:	36 feet (10.95 m)
Length:	52 feet (15.96 m)
Maximum speed:	1,550 mph (2,494 kph)
Ceiling:	65,000 feet (19,812 m)
Crew:	1
Cost:	$114 million

F/A-22 RAPTOR

The next-generation fighter plane of the U.S. Air Force

Wingspan:	45 feet (13.6 m)
Length:	62 feet (18.9 m)
Maximum speed:	1,500 mph (2,414 kph)
Ceiling:	65,000 feet (19,812 m)
Crew:	1
Cost:	$150 million

TORNADO GR4

A fighter plane used by the RAF, Germany, and Italy

Wingspan:	46 feet (13.91 m)
Length:	55 feet (16.72 m)
Maximum speed:	921 mph (1,482 kph)
Ceiling:	50,000 feet (15,240 m)
Crew:	2
Cost:	$50 million

THE M2 BRADLEY

The M2 Bradley is named after World War II general Omar Bradley. It is one of the world's most successful tanks. The M2's main mission is to transport infantry squads to key areas. Here are some of its amazing features.

A 25-mm M242 chain gun fires up to 200 rounds per minute and is accurate up to 1.5 miles (2.5 km).

A 7.62-mm M240C machine gun is located to the right of the cannon. It is equipped with antitank missiles that are capable of destroying most tanks within a range of 2.3 miles (3.75 km).

Two M257 smoke grenade launchers are each loaded with four smoke grenades.

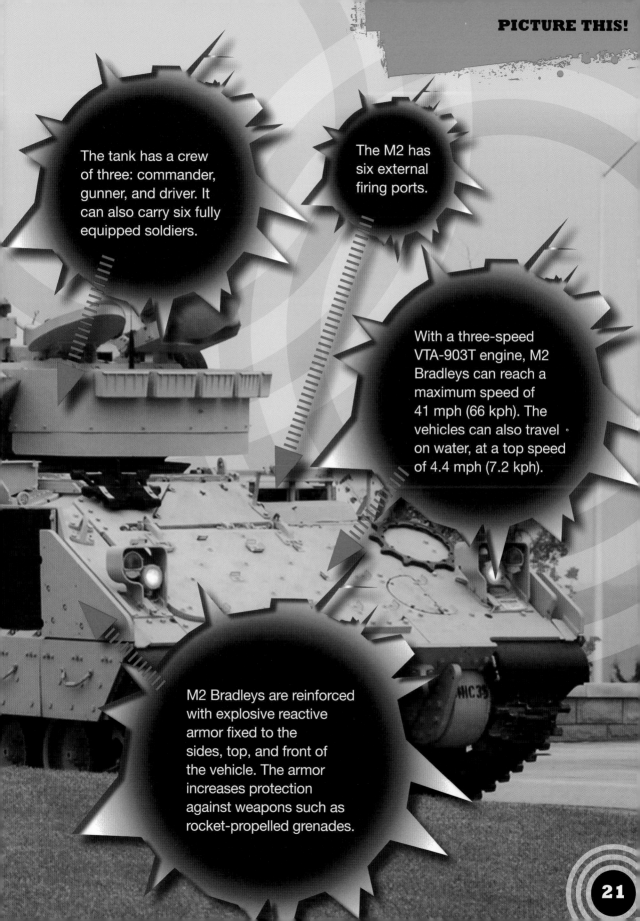

The tank has a crew of three: commander, gunner, and driver. It can also carry six fully equipped soldiers.

The M2 has six external firing ports.

With a three-speed VTA-903T engine, M2 Bradleys can reach a maximum speed of 41 mph (66 kph). The vehicles can also travel on water, at a top speed of 4.4 mph (7.2 kph).

M2 Bradleys are reinforced with explosive reactive armor fixed to the sides, top, and front of the vehicle. The armor increases protection against weapons such as rocket-propelled grenades.

HRH PRINCE HARRY

HARRY WALES

THE STATS

Name: Henry Charles Albert David Mountbatten-Windsor
Born: September 15, 1984
Place of birth: London, England
Job: Apache helicopter pilot, British Army Air Corps

MILITARY TRAINING

Prince Harry began his army career in 2005 when he joined Royal Military Academy Sandhurst in Surrey, England. Sandhurst is the British Army's officer training center. To win a place at Sandhurst, Harry had to pass a four-day assessment based on fitness and military planning. Officer Cadet Wales, as he was known, successfully completed the 44-week training.

SECRET SERVICE!

At the start of 2007, the British Ministry of Defence announced that Harry would travel with his regiment to the front line in Iraq. The plans were changed that summer when it was decided that Harry was too much of a target, a fact that could affect the safety of his regiment. However, in February 2008, the British government confirmed that Harry had been serving in Afghanistan for more than two months. For security reasons, his presence had been kept top secret.

TOP RANK

Harry was then given the rank of second lieutenant and joined the Household Cavalry's Blues and Royals regiment. After that he went to the Armour Centre in Dorset, in southwestern England, where he trained to become a tank commander.

FLYING SKILLS

In January 2008, Harry began training as a pilot with the British Army Air Corps. In March 2011, he qualified as an Apache attack helicopter pilot. Only the most talented pilots in the army are given the chance to fly Apaches, which are valued at $57 million each. In April 2011, Harry was promoted to the rank of captain and is slated to return to Afghanistan for a combat mission as early as 2012.

THE TARZAN

The Royal Marines Commandos are a small but highly trained British naval force. Royal Marines Commando training takes 32 weeks to complete. All recruits spend one week at the Marines' training center in Devon, England. On the fourth day, they attempt the Tarzan Assault Course.

HOW IT'S DONE

1. **Commando slide** (nicknamed the death slide). This rapid rope descent tests the recruit's bravery, as well as his or her head for heights.

2. **Rope walk**. The soldier travels on hands and knees along two ropes, 32 feet (10 m) off the ground and shoulder-width apart and then continues across a wobbling rope bridge.

3. **Balance test**. The recruit runs across a 16-foot (5 m) wooden bar that is just wide enough to place one foot in front of the other. Speed must be kept up, and arms are used for balance.

4. **33-foot (10 m) rope climb**. Recruits use upper-body strength to pull themselves to the top.

Essential technique

- Bravery—recruits are pushed outside their comfort zone.
- Stamina—the tests come one after the other. Recruits must stay strong to avoid making dangerous mistakes.
- Balance—recruits move at high speeds around the obstacles. If they do not stay steady, they could be seriously hurt.
- Determination—recruits need strength of will and a true desire to succeed!

33-foot (10 m) rope climb

WHY DO IT?

Royal Marines Commando training is aimed at producing well-drilled, combat-ready airmen and women. The Tarzan Assault Course is specifically designed to push recruits to their limits. When they complete the course, they are prepared as much as they will ever be for real combat conditions!

MILITARY FORCES

On the Radar looks at the world's biggest military spenders to see what they get for their money.

1. THE UNITED STATES

Annual military spending:
$650 billion
Active troops: 1.4 million
Fighter jets: 3,000
Submarines: 71
Warships: 55

2. CHINA

Annual military spending:
$96 billion
Active troops: 2.28 million
Fighter jets: 1,300
Submarines: 4
Warships: 26

3. BRITAIN

Annual military spending:
$67.6 billion
Active troops: 175,690
Fighter jets: 200
Submarines: 11
Warships: 23

4. FRANCE

Annual military spending:
$66 billion
Active troops: 352,771
Fighter jets: 300
Submarines: 10
Warships: 15

5. RUSSIA

Annual military spending:
$60 billion
Active troops: 1 million
Fighter jets: 1,200
Submarines: 24
Warships: 37

All figures
provided
are from
2009 records.

ROB HUNT

Master Sergeant Rob Hunt joined the U.S. Army while still in college. Here he tells On the Radar about his various jobs in the service.

What is your most recent job?

I've been working at the U.S. Embassy in Zagreb, Croatia, as an Operations NCO. My job there was to represent the U.S. Department of Defense and the U.S. Army to the Croatian military and to work with them on joint military exercises.

What inspired you to join the U.S. Army?

I joined the U.S. Army as a way to see the world as well as to pay for college.

What's the most interesting part of your job?

I enjoy the travel the most.

What's next for you?

My next job will move me to Fort Lewis, Washington, where I hope to become a first sergeant and be the leader of about 100 to 120 soldiers.

How many hours do you work per shift?

Ten hours is the usual shift.

What do you do in your spare time?

Same thing anyone else does—hang out with friends, watch TV, read, etc.

How's the food?

Army food isn't actually that bad. The problem is after a while you get used to it, and it all seems the same.

What skills do you need to be a linguist?

Before I became a senior leader, I was an army linguist, trained in speaking Russian and Serbo-Croatian. To be an army linguist, you have to have an easy time learning languages.

Would you recommend the army as a career?

Yes, I would recommend the army but only after you've looked really hard at it and taken the time to make sure that it's right for you. Joining the army isn't a decision to be made lightly.

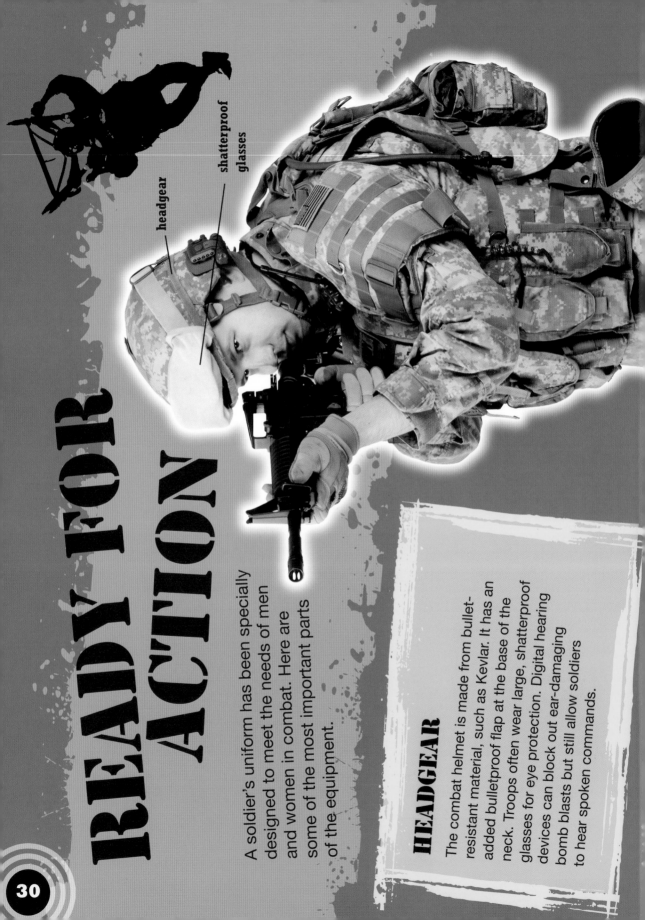

READY FOR ACTION

A soldier's uniform has been specially designed to meet the needs of men and women in combat. Here are some of the most important parts of the equipment.

headgear

shatterproof glasses

HEADGEAR

The combat helmet is made from bullet-resistant material, such as Kevlar. It has an added bulletproof flap at the base of the neck. Troops often wear large, shatterproof glasses for eye protection. Digital hearing devices can block out ear-damaging bomb blasts but still allow soldiers to hear spoken commands.

SUITED AND BOOTED

A standard Army Combat Uniform has a green-and-brown camouflage pattern that is designed to be used in woodlands, deserts, and cities. The uniforms are fire resistant and have been treated to kill mosquitoes. A bulletproof vest is also usually worn to protect vital organs, including the heart and the kidneys, from gunshots and debris from bomb blasts. Boots are tan colored and come in two weights for summer or winter conditions.

BAGS PACKED

A soldier's backpack is known as a MOLLE (pronounced Molly), which is short for Modular Lightweight Load-carrying Equipment. It holds a sleeping bag, food packets (including energy drinks and energy bars), a first-aid kit, and a large water pouch. It also holds weapons and ammo, survival materials (such as a fire-starter kit, sunscreen, and a flashlight), and communication equipment. Soldiers add personal items where there's room in the pack.

backpack
(MOLLE)

31

GET MORE INFO

Books

Donovan, Sandy. *Protecting America: A Look at the People Who Keep Our Country Safe*. Minneapolis: Lerner Publications Company, 2004. This book gives an overview of all the many groups that protect the United States from harm.

Fridell, Ron. *Military Technology*. Minneapolis: Lerner Publications Company, 2008. This book covers equipment used by the armed forces on land, at sea, and in the air.

Sutherland, Adam. *Special Forces*. Minneapolis: Lerner Publications Company, 2012. This book gives an overview of the work of special forces within the various branches of the armed services.

Sutherland, Adam. *Undercover Operations*. Minneapolis: Lerner Publications Company, 2012. Equipment and skills needed for secret ops are covered in this exciting book.

Official Websites of All the U.S. Armed Forces

U.S. Air Force
http://af.mil

U.S. Army
http://www.army.mil

U.S. Coast Guard
http://www.uscg.mil

U.S. Marine Corps
http://www.usmc.mil

U.S. Navy
http://www.navy.mil

INDEX